When God Changes Bad Into Good

Walter Zanzen

ISBN 978-1-4717-7100-2

Preface

The life of Joseph is an exciting one, and one full of unexpected situations.

God is without a doubt the One who can transform our sometimes difficult wanderings into a richly blessed experience which we would hardly dare hope for.

Walter Zanzen, head pastor of the *Eglise Evangélique de Réveil* in Geneva, is well known as a fervent student of the Word of God. He scours the depths and riches of the Scriptures.

We pray this little work will edify and encourage you, the reader.

Now may you also dive into this captivating and edifying discovery of the life of Joseph.

You will be richly blessed in doing so.

Charly Boegli
Pastor

Dear readers:

Throughout the six sermons given on the life of Joseph at the *Eglise Evangélique de Réveil* in summer 2010, the congregation's thirst and interest in the subject was tangible. Thus, I decided to make my sermon notes available, all the while maintaining their oral style, in order that the reading might kindle and stimulate in you the desire to dig a little deeper into the biblical texts. The Word of God is still living; it is the Bread of Life which nourishes our hearts and guides our choices. Truly, it is so important that we live by the godly principles which emerge in this particularly rich and instructive text. I would like to heartily thank all those who encouraged me in this endeavor, as well as all those who have read, edited, and translated this text.

Walter Zanzen, February 2011

Eglise Evangélique de Réveil
Rue du Jura 4
1201 Genève
www.eergeneve.ch

- I -

Trial is not the same as defeat

1.1 – Introduction

Let me introduce you to a character from the Bible who lived in his own era, and yet who has left a permanent impact even generations afterwards. His environment bore almost no resemblance to ours, but his example still speaks to us. Joseph, son of Jacob, never heard the Sermon on the Mount, but he applied its principles in his personal life without realizing it. He never heard Jesus say, « Love your enemies. Bless those who curse you. Do good to those who persecute you» (Matthew 5:44). He didn't know the words, « forgive us our trespasses as we forgive those who trespass against us, » (Matthew 6:12) nor « Love triumphs over judgment, » (James 2:13) and yet, he put all these passages into practice.

Well before Paul outlined the fruit of the Spirit in Galatians 5:22, Joseph was already bearing witness to them in his own life: goodness, patience, love, peace, self-control. He lived several centuries before the outpouring of the Holy Spirit at Pentecost, and yet he was recognized as a man filled with the Spirit – to the extent that even the great men of his time noticed it. This was simply the power of God at work through trials, which fashioned and ultimately transformed both his heart and his character.

Joseph preached eloquent sermons by his example and through his attitude. His whole life is an inspiration to us, and his commitment to the Lord provides encouragement when our own faith is tested. There is little question that this man has some secrets to reveal to us, and some values to impart.

1.2 – When God gives and takes away

Genesis 30:22-24

> Then God remembered Rachel; He listened to her, and enabled her to conceive. She became pregnant, and gave birth to a son. She said « God has taken away my disgrace. » She gave him the name Joseph, and said, « May the Lord add to me another son. »

There are two ideas in these verses: God took away, and God gave. Throughout his existence, Joseph's very life fluctuated between these two concepts.

The life of Jacob the patriarch is filled with upheavals worthy of a soap opera. He had two wives and two concubines, who bore him twelve sons and a daughter. Leah had seven children; Rachel had none until the day that Joseph was born, he himself the eleventh of twelve children. His was an exceptional destiny.

John Wesley, the great Methodist reformer, was the fifteenth of 19 children (10 of whom survived) ; his brother, Charles, was the 17th. Their mother, Suzanna, herself the last of 25 children, was a committed woman who took time for each of her children. When she covered her head with her apron, each child knew that they were not to disturb her – for she was praying. She had no place where she could go to be by herself, so her apron became her hiding place, where she came to call upon the Lord. This does not mean that the last-born in a family is the best, but I would dare to exhort young families: don't stop too soon! Indeed, the Lord has said to « multiply » - which indicates more than one!

Joseph is a play on words in the Hebrew language:

- *Yasaph* = God adds (another son) and
- *Asaph* = he takes away shame

Scripture devotes 13 chapters to the life of Joseph (Genesis 37 to 50), although he is not of the messianic line. Judah is of the messianic line, and is thus the ancestor of Jesus Christ, yet little is said of Judah. None of Christ's ancestors better resembles the perfect example (Christ) than Joseph, whose character and attitude so remarkably resemble, in a surprising number of ways, the One who would later appear: Jesus Christ.

You don't need to belong to a special line, to the elect, to be someone. When God has his gaze and hand upon your life, He knows what he is doing – even if the path itself is unorthodox.

Joseph's entire life fluctuated between two realities: taking away and receiving, losing and winning, leaving and returning. Even if in the eyes of men he was the « loser » for a long time, spending many years in a prison cell, forgotten and alone, ultimately the Lord was the victor in Joseph's life. God won and saved a man, a family, a clan, and many nations. Just when we seem to be the losers, God changes bad into good, loss into gain. He desires to save people through these experiences.

From Genesis to Revelation, God's intention has never changed. He desires to save, by working through our availability to him. And even if we sometimes travel paths we had not anticipated, His intention is still to save and to bring His light even to the depths of a prison, if necessary. The grand theme in Joseph's life can be summarized by this:

Romans 8:28-29

> For we know that He causes all things to work together for the good of those who love God, whom He has called according to His purpose. For those whom He foreknew, He also predestined to be conformed to the image of His son. (English Standard Version)

Working together for what end ? To be conformed to the likeness, the image, of His Son. To accomplish this, the Lord will use seemingly negative things to work together for our good: circumstances which threaten to dash our dreams and lifestyles, burden us, deeply grieve us, and doom us to « loss». But God is capable of miraculously transforming, between his holy hands, all this « bad » into something good.

1.3 – Joseph loved and hated

From his very birth, life seemed to smile upon Joseph. He had been eagerly awaited and deeply desired, as the firstborn of Rachel, Jacob's beloved. Tragically, she died during Benjamin's birth, at which point we learn that Jacob, deprived of his Rachel, transferred his affection to Joseph.

He was deeply loved by his father (and by his mother), preferred and privileged. And therein lay the rub. Favoring one child over the others is what brought about all the ensuing trouble. This set the stage for the drama which was to follow.

Astonishingly, Jacob recreated a problem which had already existed in his own family. The Bible says, « you were redeemed from the empty way of life handed down to you from your forefathers » (1 Peter 1:18). Rebecca, Jacob's mother, favored him over his brother Esau, thus creating a division in the family. This would cause him much anguish. And yet Jacob reproduced what he himself had suffered. He had not learned his lesson! He did not know what the apostle James would later say about favoritism:

James 2:9

> But if you show favoritism, you sin and are convicted by the law as lawbreakers.

Jacob had opened a breach which allowed sin to completely take over. We will see the sons of Jacob enter into bitterness, comparison, wickedness, hatred, and finally even go so far as to commit murder. This was exactly what the devil had wanted. Fortunately, God in his sovereignty redeemed all of this. However, if things repeat themselves cyclically in our lives, causing suffering, we ourselves also need to be delivered from « the empty way of life handed down to us from our forefathers. »

What a beautiful verse: « Honor your father and your mother, that it may go well with you and that you may enjoy long life on the earth» (Exodus 20:12 and Ephesians 6:2-3). God requires this of every child. But on the other hand, I do not want to reproduce that which my father or my mother passed on to me as a legacy, if it is in opposition to the kingdom of God and its values. I do not want the doors which my ancestors opened to remain that way today, allowing sin to take over. Therefore I draw near to the cross of Calvary which arrests the curses of the past. Because Jesus was cursed at the cross, he bore every curse of the law in order that I may receive the blessing of the river of life in Jesus Christ. We must have faith that *everything* was accomplished at the cross of Calvary.

Joseph was seventeen. His brothers could not tolerate that he had certain privileges (his multicolored cloak indicated an administrative position, and an absence of manual labor). He didn't dirty his hands too much, and at seventeen he was already giving orders. From a young age, he had dreamed dreams about his future: dreams which suggested a special destiny in which he would have authority, a superior position, a special ministry, and in which he would reign – even over his brothers. His brothers did not take this well. Jealous, their hearts hardened little by little. Their jealousy became hatred, and then hatred transformed into a desire for blood. What an escalation. And they went even further than that: they tried to cover up their crime. But sooner or later, all would be revealed.

Proverbs 28:13

> He who conceals his sins will not prosper. But he who confesses and renounces them finds mercy.

Joseph was put down into a well in the desert, sold to a caravan, and brought as a slave to a place far from home. He was like a lost treasure – one through whom salvation would come, but unrecognized for what he was. The brothers were the losers in this transaction. From this time on, Joseph suffered a complete stripping. Let us consider what he lost: his cloak, his brothers, his father who loved him, his country, his language, his identity, and finally his freedom. On the other hand, he maintained his faith in God, his purity, his conscience, his sensitivity, his communion with the Lord. No one could take away the Holy Spirit from him. Nothing can steal the anointing which is upon your life, and no one can threaten your destiny, because the Lord Himself stands guard.

1 Timothy 4:12

> Don't let anyone look down on you because you are young, but set an example for the believers in speech, in life, in love, in faith, and in purity.

This is what Joseph did.

Acts 23:1

> (Paul): « I have fulfilled my duty to God in all good conscience to this day. »

1 Timothy 1:18-19

> Timothy, my son, I give you this instruction in keeping with the prophecies once made about you, so that by following them you may fight the good fight, holding on to faith and a good conscience. Some have rejected these and so have shipwrecked their faith.

Joseph guarded his heart and his conscience above all else. He did not become a hardened, indifferent, uncompromising man during all these years, but maintained a sensitive and humble heart, which still knew how to grieve.

1.4 – God was with Joseph

Genesis 39:1-6

> Now Joseph had been brought down to Egypt, and Potiphar, an officer of Pharaoh, the captain of the guard, an Egyptian, had bought him from the Ishmaelites who had brought him down there. The LORD was with Joseph, and he became a successful man, and he was in the house of his Egyptian master. His master saw that the LORD was with him and that

> the LORD caused all that he did to succeed in his hands. So Joseph found favor in his sight and attended him, and he made him overseer of his house and put him in charge of all that he had. From the time that he made him overseer in his house and over all that he had the LORD blessed the Egyptian's house for Joseph's sake; the blessing of the LORD was on all that he had, in house and field. So he left all that he had in Joseph's charge.

The Scriptures highlight the positive: adding. Men had done the cutting off and removing, and now God was beginning to masterfully add back in. « The LORD was with Joseph, his master saw that the LORD was with him » and the Lord blessed the entire house of his master.

Proverbs 10:22

> The blessing of the LORD makes rich.

When I am blessed, I am made rich. Only the blessing of God can do this. God's intention is to come down to Egypt; he loves this people and this country (Isaiah 19) ; he desires that the Egyptians see proof of his existence and his blessing.

The Lord desires to come into certain places to furnish the proof of his goodness and favor, and to reveal himself. For this he needs his children. He needs your life. The place where you are may not be the place you would have chosen, and may not be the ideal place, but the plan of God is to bring to this place a revelation of his presence. God would like to inhabit this place where we are, by his blessing and his presence.

1.5 – Darkness is cast down before the favor of God

This favor aroused the ill will of Joseph's brothers, who were carried away by carnal behavior, and who could not accept the dreams of their younger brother which were, nevertheless, spiritual (misinterpreted, certainly, but spiritual). Carnal man, in his human reasoning, opposes himself to the working out of the perfect plan of God, and to the favor of God which comes upon someone. When a piece of God's presence arrives in an obscure place, the darkness reacts, arousing conflict and incomprehension by carnal man, and unleashes the anger of the devil. In the life of one person, the larger God's favor is, the more the darkness is disturbed, and the more powerful the temptations to lose God's favor become.

1.6 - Joseph maintained his relationship with God, no matter the cost

Despite the painful rejection of his own family, Joseph did not lose the favor of God upon his life. Though deprived of his cloak and the love of his father, and far from his country, – he did not lose his communion with God. Likewise, he did not lose his spiritual gift, even upon hitting rock bottom in the depths of prison after being slandered. In this place too, his spiritual gifts were made manifest, and he interpreted the dream of two supporting characters (Pharaoh's chief baker and chief cupbearer). Filled with the Holy Spirit, Joseph let himself be used by Him. Yet the baker and cupbearer forgot about him, their well-meaning words dissipated, and their promises faded away, unkept. In the depths of his prison cell, the spirit of God was both with him and at work. God encouraged him « I have not taken my Holy Spirit from you. Let me act in your life, and don't give up hope. » One could certainly ask: « Why all these injustices ? Why this mess ? » Trials can destabilize even the faithful, and the temptation to give up can grow stronger.

1.7 – What does the Bible say about this time of testing ?

Psalm 105:17-20

> And he sent a man before them, Joseph, sold as a slave. They bruised his feet with shackles, his neck was put in irons: **till what he foretold came to pass, till the word of the LORD** proved him true. The king sent and released him, the ruler of the people set him free.

The trials in which we sometimes find ourselves are subordinate to the word of God:when He says « stop, » « that's far enough, » the trial must release its grip, because God is in charge. Then the losses will be transformed into profits, into benefits. Let us rejoice in the sovereignty of God. Trials come to an end at His command.

1 Corinthians 10:13

> No temptation has seized you except what is common to man: and God is faithful, He will not let you be tempted beyond what you can bear. But when you are tempted, he will also provide a **way out** so that you can **stand up under it**.

Here is a verse that we would all do well to memorize, because we will all be confronted with trials at one time or another. Trial knocks at our door without asking if it may enter or not, but invites itself in. And yet, God watches over this by his sovereign command, and his word which will be brought to pass. He declares « this far and no further. »

1.8 – After loss comes gain

Only two years later, the cupbearer remembered Joseph and spoke of him to Pharaoh, who had had two dreams which no one could interpret. Thus it was that, in a single day, Joseph's destiny changed. Every closed door was suddenly opened. All those years of grief and injustice, deprivation and solitude, are transformed into restoration, glory, promotion, victory, and one blessing heaped upon another. Joseph, once rejected, is welcomed as a savior by the entire country. They saw who he was: a man of God, a man of wisdom and discernment, who possessed within himself the Spirit of God. They placed their trust in him immediately.

Genesis 41:38

> And Pharaoh said unto his servants, « Can we find such a one as this is, a man in whom the Spirit of God is ? »

Thirteen years of suffering had taught him, shaped him, and left him humble; his heart had retained its tenderness.

1.9 – Was Joseph sold or sent ?

Psalm 105:17-24

> And he **sent** a man before them – Joseph, **sold** as a slave.

Was Joseph sold or sent ? His brothers and circumstances sold him. He felt betrayed, exploited, forgotten. But God says, « No, that is not how I see things. I sent you before your brothers. » Even his brothers would one day follow after him. God sent Joseph BEFORE his brothers. He prepared the place to which his brothers would come; he welcomed them and forgave them. Sin sold Joseph to the injustice and wickedness which nearly broke him, but God was watching over him. No one can wreck our destiny.

Joseph would later say, in

Genesis 45:5, 7-8

> And now do not be distressed and do not be angry with yourselves for selling me here, because it was to

> save lives that God sent me here ahead of you. But God sent me ahead of you to preserve for you a remnant on earth and to save your lives by a great deliverance. So then, it was not you who sent me here, but God.

He is so conscious of having been sent, by God, that he is free of all hatred. He could have said, « these brothers shattered my life, stole my youth, robbed me of my father and caused everyone grief. » But he is conscious of having been sent in order to be able to welcome them and love them on that day when they finally arrived.

1.10 - How do we deal with trials ?

What is our position: do we know ourselves to be sent of God, or do we feel we have been sold by forces stronger than ourselves? Do we find ourselves thinking: « sold, betrayed, exploited, unjustly treated by people and even my brothers, society, or by one more powerful than me. My life is condemned, my plans destroyed » ? Or can we believe that God will cause all things to work together for our good, that he will use this to accomplish His purpose ? We have the choice to view our lives through one of these two lenses. Joseph made a choice: he saw the hand of God, he knew how to guard his heart, he accepted God's divine instruction, he humbled himself beneath the sovereign will, and he refused to harden his heart although he had the opportunity to do so. In the end, his brothers would be touched by his outstanding character

- II -

Temptation is not the same as giving in to sin

2.1 – Genesis 39:5-20

5 From the time that he made him overseer in his house and over all that he had, **the Lord blessed** the Egyptian's house for Joseph's sake; **the blessing of the Lord** was on all that he had, in house and field. 6 So he left all that he had in Joseph's charge, and because of him he had no concern about anything but the food he ate. Now Joseph was handsome in form and appearance. 7 And after a time his master's wife cast her eyes on Joseph and said, "Lie with me." 8 But **he refused** and said to his master's wife, "Behold, because of me my master has no concern about anything in the house, and he has put everything that he has in my charge. 9 He is not greater in this house than I am, nor has he kept back anything from me except you, because you are his wife. **How then can I do this great wickedness and sin against God?**" 10 And as she spoke to Joseph day after day, he would not listen to her, to lie beside her or to be with her. 11 But one day, when he went into the house to do his work and none of the men of the house was there in the house, 12 she caught him by his garment, saying, "Lie with me." But **he left his garment in her hand and fled** and got out of the house. 13 And as soon as she saw

> that he had left his garment in her hand and had
> fled out of the house, 14 she called to the men of
> her household and said to them, "See, he has
> brought among us a Hebrew to laugh at us. He came
> in to me to lie with me, and I cried out with a loud
> voice. 15 And as soon as he heard that I lifted up my
> voice and cried out, he left his garment beside me
> and fled and got out of the house." 16 Then she laid
> up his garment by her until his master came home,
> 17 and she told him the same story, saying, "The
> Hebrew servant, whom you have brought among us,
> came in to me to laugh at me. 18 But as soon as I
> lifted up my voice and cried, he left his garment
> beside me and fled out of the house." 19 As soon as
> his master heard the words that his wife spoke to
> him, "This is the way your servant treated me," his
> anger was kindled. 20 And Joseph's master took him
> and put him into the prison, the place where the
> king's prisoners were confined, and he was there in
> prison.

Joseph's trials seem almost surreal. With God, trials are never meant to destroy us, overwhelm us, or wipe us out completely, but to train and shape us (1 Corinthians 10 :13). Thus it is that God permits us to undergo painful experiences – sometimes long and difficult ones – but Christians always receive the inner strength to endure. Something supernatural carries us during times of testing. There are some things which we can only learn through pressure and suffering. Even Jesus had to experience this.

Hebrews 5:8

> Even though Jesus was God's son, he learned obedience by the things he suffered.

Joseph conquered his trials one by one. The strength of his soul enabled him to say « it was not you that sent me here, but God. » He ultimately saw the big picture of God's marvelous and mysterious plan for him and his family. Joseph had one conviction: he would remain in the Lord's hands, whatever the cost.

Blessing will follow if you remain faithful where you have been sent, regardless of the circumstances. This blessing will touch others, and they will notice it, but this blessing will also release adversity.

2.2 – The three phases of Joseph's life during the time of testing

Phase 1: Prosperity

Joseph entered the house of Potiphar against his will – it was not his choice, but he was led there in spite of himself. It was God's choice: divine election. Joseph resolved to serve in this place where he had landed; he would not rebel, but would submit himself in his circumstances, confident that God had a sovereign and superior plan.

With this in mind, let us consider the story of Naaman's slave, the little maid who waited on his wife, who served her master and desired his good. (See 2 Kings 5.)

God blessed this righteous attitude, her humble and devoted service in a setting that she would not have chosen. How can we know if we are sent somewhere by God, or not ? If we have been, then blessing will also appear sooner or later, even in less-than-ideal circumstances. As already stated, the Lord sees the dark places, and desires to illumine them, and to touch those around us, in order that they too might taste and see that He is good.

Joseph was young – only 17 years old – but already prosperity had become his companion. He had no power at all, and yet everything he undertook succeeded. If God is with you, He will cause you to prosper even if you are not powerful or well-known. Even if you possess nothing, God's blessing will appear.

The secret of Joseph's victory lay in the fact that he treasured the presence of God. No one can take away the presence of God from you, if you choose to abide with the Lord. Seven times in chapter 39, Genesis states that « the LORD was with him » or « the hand of God was upon him. » After having lost everything, Joseph took courage once more. He had seen that the Lord did bless. He would live blamelessly in the house of Potiphar, with integrity and righteousness in his solitude. In so doing, he chose not to follow in the footsteps of his father Jacob, who had been a sly man, and full of tricks.

Phase 2: Temptation

God's blessing enrages the enemy. The Bible introduces the next step with these words:« after these things. » There is a pivotal moment where prosperity is followed by a time of testing and temptation. The Bible affirms that even the most righteous and holy of men was tempted one day. Temptation befalls not only the young: it comes across the path of every Christian. It makes incredible, alluring propositions, and digs a pit before us. Its goal is to remove you from the presence of God. Temptation comes when we're least expecting it.

Someone had seen Joseph (« *the woman cast her eyes upon Joseph»).* Potiphar's wife had noticed something interesting, appealing, and attractive in him. The moment of proposition arrived! She had concocted her plan over the course of some time, and had followed him with her eyes for a while – perhaps even without him noticing. Temptation was already in action – it had gone before Joseph and was going to choose the most favorable moment to trap this righteous man.

James 1:13-15

> When tempted, no one should say, « God is tempting me. » For God cannot be tempted by evil, nor does He tempt anyone; but each one is tempted when, by his own evil desire, he is dragged away and enticed. Then, after desire has conceived, it brings forth sin. And sin, when it is full-grown, gives birth to death.

It is important to note that temptation is not sin. When I let myself be carried away by my thoughts, if I play with the idea of temptation, I go down a dangerous path. Temptation must be conquered by taking a firm stance, by a determined will, with the conviction and strength to **not** acquiesce, to **not** proceed any further. Let us observe :

- Lust begins in our senses – it is the attraction of the flesh.

- It is said that Joseph was handsome. He may have been quite a head-turner! He certainly exhibited a powerful sort of magnetism upon at least one woman. When Potiphar was no longer particularly interesting for his wife, she said to herself « my husband is never there, he doesn't take care of me, he doesn't listen to me anymore, I know him too well. » And thus it happened that she saw in Joseph the « perfect man » who could bring to her everything her husband no longer could. This is the trap.

- The demand made by Potiphar's wife is clear and straightforward:*Lie with me!* This temptation is as old as the world – that of sexual sin, forbiden sexuality not authorized by the Lord. (Sexuality is a good and beautiful thing, designed by the Creator, but it must be experienced within the framework which the Lord has designated for blessing to result from it – that is, the covenant of marriage.)

- Joseph's response was equally clear: *he refused...day by day.* And then finally, *she caught him.*

Some temptations are insistent and perseverant, returning regularly, and we must assume our position against them every single time. The woman's proposition came so close to Joseph that she ultimately managed to seize his very garment. She wanted to wear him down, whatever the cost.

The text reveals to us that Potiphar's wife was not in love, but impassioned. What's the difference ? Love means giving one's life to the other, and seeking the other's good – which bears absolutely no resemblance to the passion described here. Passion wants to obtain at any price, achieve its objective, and realize a desire – a fantasy.

When Joseph unequivocally refused, this passion instantly dissipated and transformed into a criminally destructive will. The woman wanted to avenge herself and destroy Joseph. She injured him as a serpent attacks its victim, and had no qualms about betraying him with a lie.

It is crucial to learn how to rule over our passions, and to discipline ourselves. This is an indispensable exercise to experience success and protection in one's life.

Phase 3: Victory

Where did Joseph's determination come from ? It was found in his faithfulness. He refused to betray his employer. He said at the given time, « you do not belong to me, you are my boss's wife. » He is also faithful to his conscience, saying « my spirit and my convictions will not permit me to do such a thing. » To go further would mean trespassing an inner boundary, breaking it, and – in so doing – muffling his conscience. Finally, he is faithful to the Lord, because he fears God. In verse 9, he says, « *How then can I do this great wickedness, and sin against God ?* » For Joseph, the word of God is too precious and important. It is his guard rail. He simply cannot transgress this, because he fears the Lord. The plan of God is too precious to be dishonored in this way.

Isaiah 66:2

> This is the one who I esteem: he who is humble and contrite in spirit, and **trembles at my word**.

The day after he had sinned with Bathsheba, David was convicted by the Holy Spirit and declared:

Psalm 51:4

> Against you, **you only**, have I sinned, and done what is evil in your sight, so that you are proved right when you speak, and justified when you judge.

He understood that to have given in to temptation was a sin against God (as well as against Bathsheba).

If we want to conquer temptation, we must get out in front of it – that is, we must be decided and determined *in advance.* We must be on guard at all times, which means paying careful attention to our relationship with

God. We should under no circumstances peddle away our conscience nor our purity.

Let us remember Daniel, who resolved not to defile himself (Daniel 1:8), and also Samson (Judges 13 and afterwards). The latter, gifted with supernatural strength by the spirit of God, would be made weak – not at the beginning of his misadventures with women (at which point he was already placing himself in danger) but on the day when he broke his final vow. Before breaking his vow as a Nazirite (which was an external sign of consecration), he had already broken a whole series of internal vows within his heart. He was already engaged in multiple compromises, and it was this which had placed him in danger. At the moment when he believed himself to still be strong, he no longer was.

We have to nurture and strengthen our commitment to not injure the Lord or run counter to His will, nor to grieve Him. Committing fornication or adultery is sin. Let this be perfectly clear:it is right to keep oneself sexually pure for marriage – this is what God requires of the Christian. Some may say, « why wait ? We'll get married later. » The decision to keep oneself sexually pure for marriage is proof that we honor what God honors – the holy covenant, instituted by the Creator. I would invite the young, and the less young, to resolve to stand firm and not commit fornication, nor adultery, both of which are clearly called sin by the Scriptures.

Joseph had to take a stand within himself first

If we want to be a man or woman of God at 30 or 50 years old, we have to be one at 17 or 25. May we, today, be strong in the face of the multiple temptations which our society proposes. To be trustworthy before others, we must first be so alone (removed from everyone, no one would have known !). At any rate, God sees. *No, I will not commit sin before the Lord.*

We cannot live reprehensible lives in private, and then develop an anointed ministry in public, because the anointing of a ministry begins in private – otherwise a scandal is sure to erupt. Even if our generation is tempted like no other, as Christians we maintain a clear and radical position: « *I choose to be a person, a young person, who will remain pure with regards to my sexuality in this overly sexualized world which at every moment offers propositions which would open the door to temptations.* » God help us !

Joseph did not converse with temptation

If we enter into discussion, the battle is already half lost. Joseph does not respond to the object of temptation – he avoids it, flees from it, and puts distance between it and him. He doesn't believe himself to be stronger than he is! The thought must be crystal-clear: « *this person belongs to someone* » (to her husband, to his wife, to the Lord, or – if single – to a future spouse.)

2.3 - Conclusion

For Joseph, holiness was not just a word. He loved purity, and he had to pay the price for that. This love for holiness should live within us. What is the value of holiness in our life ? Is it an accessory, or a priority ?

1 Peter 1:16

> Be ye holy, for I am holy.

Joseph's determination was his salvation, as it necessitated his flight from temptation. Sometimes we must flee incessant temptation.

2 Timothy 2:22

> Flee also youthful lusts.

If you have failed, your conscience accuses you and you carry a burden. It is never too late to return to God. God loves us and wants to lift up the one who has fallen.

1 John 1:9

> If we confess our sins, He is faithful and just to forgive us our sins, and to cleanse us from all unrighteousness.

God raises up the sinner through confession. Take a decision like Joseph: *I will be holy, I will live in victory, and I will not lose my life by sullying it or ruining it.*

Genesis chapter 38, placed in the middle of the story of Joseph, is there to show us of the tremendous disorder created by the uncontrolled sexuality of Judah. It is a must read!

- III -

Affliction is not the same as impotence

Genesis 39:20-23

> And Joseph's master took him, and put him into the prison, a place where the king's prisoners were bound: and he was there in the prison. But the LORD was with Joseph, and showed him mercy, and gave him favor in the sight of the keeper of the prison. And the keeper of the prison committed to Joseph's hand all the prisoners that were in the prison; and whatsoever they did there, he was the doer of it. The keeper of the prison looked not to any thing that was under his hand: because the LORD was with him, and that which he did, the LORD made it to prosper.

3.1 – His soul was afflicted, but alive

Psalm 105:17-18

> And he sent a man before them, Joseph, sold as a slave. They bruised his feet with shackles, his neck was put in irons.

Literally, « he was put in iron » or, more precisely, « iron came upon his soul. » This reveals the brand of deep inner suffering Joseph experienced during his captivity. It was God who chose this path for him (« He sent... ») ; we would never choose such a path of our own accord! Joseph was arrested physically by the chains of his prison cell, but things were going on deep within him too. Was he still conscious of the presence of God, and of the fact that « all things work together for his good? » Probably not!

You may be strong in the face of trials, but at some point you feel that your soul is being squeezed, constricted, that you're suffocating, and you no longer understand anything. When trials seem to repeat themselves; when rejection is heaped upon rejection, injustice upon injustice, and disappointment upon disappointment; it may be just one final straw which breaks your soul. You're disgusted, and questions begin to creep in: « What could I have done to deserve this? » Even praying can become difficult.

Upon interviewing French journalist Roger Auque, who had been a hostage in Beirut – released on November 27, 1987 after 319 days in captivity – he was asked about his regrets. He responded, « I'm going to tell you something which will surprise you. This captivity was necessary for me to come to know God and his existence. »

3.2 – His faith was tested, but steadfast

Can you still believe in your dreams from the depths of a prison cell? Are they completely lost and beyond any hope of resurrection? "Did I really hear the Lord? Was it really You who spoke to me? Was it not just my imagination?" Reality cries that everything is going wrong. Doubt tries to worm its way in, but let us not forget that Reality is not Truth. Truth is always what God has said and decided. We have observed that Joseph's dreams are exactly what would incite the opposition of his brothers. It was this spiritual dynamic and the call and presence of God within the life of Joseph, which provoked and fed their hatred. Because of this, an invisible wall was erected between him and his brothers. We see Joseph separate himself from the world of his brothers (along with their rivalries, criticisms, jealousy, and ill-will) and withstand the pressure they put on him.

Joseph was filled with an inner peace, knowing by faith that what God had showed him would come to pass. By faith he was sustained and supported. God can neither lie nor himself be misled. When God gives us a spiritual vision, it will be examined – or « put in irons » – and tested, and it is precisely at this moment that our faith is shown to be like a well-planted tree which stands up straight and tall, thanks to the depth of its root structure.

Hebrews 11:1

> Faith is the assurance of things hoped for, the certainty of what we do not see.

The fulfillment of things hoped for may come later than desired, but it will come!

3.3 – His witness was vibrant

The Bible declares that Joseph was *sent* by God to Potiphar, and now he is *sent* to prison! The multicolored coat that Joseph wore was like the Chanel *haute couture* of his day ; he had received it from his father. His new masters would dress him in a simple, new outfit – that of a slave, a servant of Potiphar – and then others would unjustly array him in the uniform of a prison inmate (imagine stripes or solid orange fabric). Even « de-classed » and stripped by men, Joseph nevertheless retained his value in the eyes of God. Perhaps you may be « de-classed » by people one day. They will remove different titles from you, but they will never be able to threaten your value. Even dressed as a prisoner, Joseph is in the hand of God.

What they said of him in the house of Potiphar, they also said of him in prison. It was the same refrain:*God is with him – the Lord has caused him to succeed.* Blessing and divine favor followed him. When our soul is alive, and we stay connected to the Lord without allowing anything whatsoever to break our communion with him, the same refrain rings true in our life: that of blessing. Blessing accompanied him – it was always around the corner, unable to be restrained from following him wherever he went. When people saw Joseph, they saw that God was with him.

1 Peter 4:19

> Therefore, let those who suffer according to the will of God commit their souls to the faithful Creator while doing good.

It is not easy to do good while suffering. We have a tendancy to fold in on ourselves and to want to take care of our own needs. But Joseph was attentive to others, all the while suffering himself; in this way he was a type of Christ.

Acts 10:38

> How God anointed Jesus of Nazareth with the Holy Ghost and with power: who went about doing good, and healing all that were oppressed of the devil; for God was with him.

The challenge is to do good where we are, where we have been placed. Joseph's work was not lost because he found himself in the depths of prison. He practiced his ministry where he was, by making himself available to his Lord. A divine vocation can be exercised regardless of the circumstances. Don't wait for the circumstances to be ideal or perfect to begin serving. Choose to serve and to be a good example there where you've been planted.

3.4 – Trials prepare us

1 Peter 5:10

> In his kindness God called you to share in his eternal glory by means of Christ Jesus. So after you have suffered a little while, he will restore, support, and

strengthen you, and he will place you on a firm foundation.

1 Peter 1:7

Faith that has been tested is precious.

We don't often define trials in this way: « The greater the task God calls me to, the more time he takes to prepare me for it. » Joseph would be still more stripped, forgotten (going from one master to another and from one injustice to another), and made to sink lower and lower as he went through God's « forge. »

Steel must be tempered in order to be made into a useful tool. The metal must undergo the trial of tempering, which consists of heating the metal until it is white-hot, and then abruptly thrusting it into cold water. Once pulled back out, it hardens. This process is repeated several times, alternating between extreme heat and brutal cold. The succession of hot and cold gives the metal a unique structure which endows it with properties of strength and resistance.

Without knowing it, Joseph resembled Jesus the Saviour (who experienced injustice, rejection, abandonment, the loneliness of trials, misunderstanding, subjection to false witness, and betrayal by those closest to him). God had great plans for his servant Joseph, the future saviour of his people; overall, his time of preparation lasted for thirteen years. He was like a precious gemstone, fashioned by expert hands.

3.5 – Trials test us

Deuteronomy 8:2

> Remember how the Lord your God led you through the wilderness for these forty years, humbling you and testing you to prove your character, and to find out whether or not you would obey his commands.

God permits trials in order to bring to light what is going on deep within us. He wants to see our deepest motivations, to test our values. He wants to know where our integrity lies. Trials create a tension: give up, or resist discouragement; stand firm, or give in to rebellion. Our attitudes and behaviors are tested. For example:« am I prepared to discipline myself and remain sexually pure, and to persevere on the right path? This time is necessary for the training of our character.

We don't enthusiastically welcome this regimen, but it is nevertheless part of the path which the Lord has planned for us. We tend to want to « trim » or « shorten » our cross in order to make it lighter. At the risk of sounding repetitive: trials are an agent which reveals who we are, and which bring to light what lies in the depths of our heart. This is a time of preparation for a grand mission, so let us take courage !

Genesis 40:1-14 and 20-23

It is astonishing to compare this story with that of Jesus. In his unjust condemnation by men, Joseph encountered two accused, condemned men. To the one would be revealed his redemption; to the other, his death. This reminds us of the two criminals crucified on either side of Jesus. Jesus was the one crucified in the middle, and he announced heaven to the one. To the one who said to him, « remember me » Jesus said « Truly I say to you, today you shall be with me in Paradise » (Luke 23 :43), but the other would die in his sins.

Let's come back to the story of Joseph. The two men in prison are in despair. What will grant them comfort ? Joseph is there, sharing their trial, having lost none of his spiritual fervor himself, but he is filled with the Holy Spirit and attentive to His voice. He takes care of his relationship with God, and this above everything else. Thus, he is able to help those whose trials he shares. He is able to comfort them.

Around us there are so many souls who have no hope, who are distraught and panicked. « What will become of me ? What will happen to him ? » These men are in need of interaction with Christians who are assured of God's presence; who radiate peace and serenity; who have this peaceful confidence within them. Their testimony is received because they are in the same situation – which is not to say in the same mess – as the others.

Joseph is forgotten by men

This cupbearer of the king – lucky, and encouraged by Joseph's words – would quickly forget him. He would neither remember him, nor show him any recognition. Have you ever been the victim of a broken promise ? Well, Joseph understands. Jesus understands. When the consequences are insignificant, it is not too serious, but when being forgotten means having your time in prison unjustly prolonged by two years or more! Joseph could have become bitter, rebellious, vindictive, but he didn't.

So many people feel forgotten by their own, and some even feel forgotten by the church, the family of God. They say, for example, « No one takes notice of my suffering, no one sees my loneliness or my problems. I'm not taken seriously. » Or even « No one recognizes my gift or my ministry. » Joseph acts in righteousness, with a right attitude ; his life is a good testimony, and he is innocent. And yet, despite having such a powerful gift, he is forgotten!

Time passes. The years tick by, and his youth passes him by in the depths of a prison. Some of his most promising years were wasted, pointlessly lost, because of one wicked person's slanderous lie.

Hebrews 6 :10

> For God is not unjust so as to overlook your work and the love that you have shown for his name in serving the saints, as you still do.

Forgotten by men, but prepared by the Lord

God knows what He's doing. He takes care of those lives entrusted to Him. No, Joseph's life is not ruined ; God is capable of changing bad into good. With great secrecy, He is at work fashioning a precious jewel – and this, far from the gaze and activities of men! In the depths of a prison cell, God was at work preparing Joseph's future. In fact, He was preparing the future of his chosen people. With his own blessed hands God caught up Joseph's heart and soul. If he was forgotten, unjustly treated, and made to suffer pointlessly at the hands of men, for the Lord he was in a phase of preparation, set apart in the most secret of places.

2 Corinthians 4:16-18

> So we do not lose heart. Though our outer self is wasting way, our inner self is being renewed day by day. For this light and momentary affliction is preparing for us an eternal weight of glory beyond all comparison, as we look not to the things that are seen but to the things that are unseen. For the things that are seen are transient, but the things that are unseen are eternal.

Psalm 138:7

> Though I walk in the midst of trouble, You preserve my life.

3.7 – And in God's timing Joseph was restored

In His own timing, as Psalm 105 says, when God said « stop, » Joseph was summoned. Two whole years had passed, and then in an instant the cupbearer remembered Joseph. Pharaoh needed him; God needed him. Upon the life of Joseph rested such an anointing of the Holy Spirit that everyone was convinced of the truth which flowed from Joseph's mouth. Everyone took him seriously. His gift was made manifest as he interpreted the dream before people who had absolutely no interest in the God of Israel. And he did it with such anointing that Pharaoh was convinced that there stood before him a servant of the all-powerful God, and – what was more – a man highly qualified to oversee something important. From the very lowest position, Joseph ascended to the highest. This was the result of perseverence and a right attitude in the midst of testing. Let us not lose heart !

Genesis 41:15-16

> And Pharaoh said to Joseph, « I have had a dream, and there is no one who can interpret it. I have heard it said of you that when you hear a dream you can interpret it. » Joseph answered Pharaoh, « It is not in me; God will give Pharaoh a favorable answer. »

Genesis 41:37-39

> This proposal pleased Pharaoh and all his servants. And Pharaoh said to his servants, « Can we find a man like this, in whom is the Spirit of God ? » Then Pharaoh said to Joseph, « Since God has shown you all this, there is none so discerning and wise as you are. »

Made fruitful

Genesis 41:50-52

> Before the years of famine came, two sons were born to Joseph. Asenath, the daughter of Potiphera priest of On, bore them to him. Joseph called the name of the firstborn Manasseh. « For, » he said, « God has made me forget all my hardship and all my father's house. » The name of the second he called Ephraim, « For God has made me fruitful in the land of my affliction. »

Have you noticed the names that Joseph gave his sons ? Ephraim and Manasseh. God destines us to bear fruit in the country of affliction, to never be sterile no matter where we are.

John 15:2-4

> Every branch in me that does not bear fruit he takes away, and every branch that does bear fruit he prunes, that it may bear more fruit. Already you are clean because of the word that I have spoken to you. Abide in me, and I in you. As the branch cannot bear fruit by itself, unless it abides in the vine, neither can you, unless you abide in me.

Lord, I do still want to be used by you, even if I am not in a place I like very much, or in pleasant circumstances. What I've had to live through has been useful, necessary for me to become who I am today. I bow myself beneath your sovereign hand, Father, understanding that this is part of your training plan for me. You know why and for whom you are doing this. Amen.

- IV -

A painful past need no longer destroy: the meeting with his brothers

Acts 7:9-10

> And the patriarchs, moved with envy, sold Joseph into Egypt. But God was with him, and delivered him out of all his afflictions.

A busy Christian walking down the corridor of a Paris metro ran into another commuter, just as hurried as she. Politely she apologized and asked him to forgive her, but the man turned around, looked at her, and retorted, « These days we don't forgive anymore – we kill. »

Fortunately, Joseph did not adopt this behavior. He was probably tormented by his injuries, asking himself all the usual questions, but he was able to rise above the hurt they caused him. He was able to overcome his traumatic experiences by the grace of God, because God had pulled him out of his trials. Joseph was able to let go of his past, putting it to death, but at the end what would be the state of his heart, his soul ? Let us remember that we can easily kill with the sword of the mouth, or with the bitter venom of the tongue. He could have made his brothers pay for their wrongdoing, but Joseph lived by a different set of principles which we would do well to remember.

4.1 - He chose to keep his heart pure and to maintain communion with God

The Bible says over and over again that « God was with him. » Regardless of the cost, Joseph kept a close relationship with the Lord. He protected this communion with God, and safeguarded it. He never permitted the enemy to use adversity to cut him off from the Lord. He never permitted the enemy to succeed in persuading him to this end by saying « you see everything that's happening to you – all this injustice. God has forgotten you, and nothing is going right, despite your piety, despite your faith. You have the right to shake your fist at the heavens, to react, to take vengeance. You have the right. »

Joseph did not permit this type of reaction to invade his soul. Don't allow the enemy to meddle in your relationship with God. It is the most precious thing you have. The enemy is jealous of this relationship, and he will do whatever he can to erect a wall between you and God. He knows that it's thus that you are weakened, and put on a slippery slope; that you're in great danger and that your testimony no longer has an impact.

4.2 – He chose to remain available within the hands of the Lord

Do you like to talk about Jesus when you're not feeling well, when you are grieving or struggling with pain?

Sometimes it is precisely when we are at our lowest that the perfect opportunity to witness presents itself. But due to the grief and trials, we feel empty, demotivated, and less- or even un-available because we are so focused on ourselves. It is precisely there where the challenge lies. In prison Joseph learned that it is « better to take refuge in the LORD than to trust in men. » He had counted on the help of the cupbearer, who forgot about him. Yet the cupbearer too was in the hand of the Lord, and his memory was suddenly refreshed, at just the right moment, in God's timing. Yes, the time of fulfillment does arrive.

After seven years of prosperity, the storage houses of Egypt were overflowing with wheat; then came the seven years of bitter famine. Joseph, rehabilitated, respected, and recognized by everyone throughout the land, was in charge of the country. Thus it was that, at the peak of his restoration, his past came back to him, full circle.

4.3 – One day his brothers reappeared. But why ?

Psalm 105 :17

> *Joseph was sent before his brothers* (but they would follow).

The famine pushed them out of their country, and into Egypt. God allowed this meeting to take place between Joseph and his brothers, for multiple reasons.

First, God knew the questions which haunted Joseph. He had a family – his wife and two sons, Manasseh and Ephraim. He seemed happy, but the absence of his family in the land of Canaan was very real. Perhaps he felt an emptiness, although twenty years had already passed by since the day that he had been sold. His wife might have said to him, « Joseph, what do you mean by this far-off look, this nostalgia? Are my love and our two children not enough ? » But all the splendor of Egypt could not cover up the absence of his family's faces, and the void which remained. He said to himself, « What has become of my father and my little brother, and the others? I would like to see them again. » Joseph could hardly be comforted.

Genesis 42:7

Joseph saw his brothers, and he knew them.

And in an instant, his entire past came back to him. Yet, Joseph had forgotten (Genesis 41 :51). Can we really forget the offenses of the past ? Offense can cling to our memory like a tick. It feeds on the blood and vitality of its victim, and the wound becomes infected. The offense refuses to be forgotten, and it evolves little by little into rancor and bitterness. Meanwhile, the Christian knows that he should not seek vengeance, and prays « forgive us our trespasses as we forgive those who trespass against us. » Herein lies the crisis. I must forgive, but I simply cannot.

Verse 51 tells us that **God** had caused him to forget. Of ourselves, we would never be able to forget such a violent trauma; it would seem, humanly speaking, impossible. But someone helped him during these twenty years:the Lord. Joseph refused to dwell on the wrong that had been done to him. He refused to allow the memory to return to his mind endlessly. He had entrusted all this to the Lord. It was the Lord who had put his hand of protection around Joseph's vulnerable soul, to keep it safe and to heal it. He had refused this « compulsion to remember, » which would have been so destructive, harmful, and dangerous. Because of this choice to forget, he could flourish, grow, learn, and be made useful in the hands of God.

Only the Lord can help us to forget offenses, insofar as we decide to work with Him and choose to forgive. If it was God who helped him to forget, it was Joseph himself who also chose to turn over certain pages. He called his son Ephraim (« God has caused me to be fruitful »), thus demonstrating that his life was by no means over.

If you desire your life to recover its strength like a fresh springtime full of hope; to have a life which bears fruit and leaves a legacy; it is necessary to take this step towards forgiveness, with God's help. If we have dried-out, unproductive lives, it is because we are clinging to the past, refusing to let go of an offense. A desire for vengeance will always lead to dryness, famine, unfruitfulness, and – in the long term – death of the soul. Let Manasseh and Ephraim be born in the depths of your heart.

4.4 – The decision to meet them

Joseph had a choice. He was powerful, and he could either ignore his brothers when they arrived, avenge himself, or meet with them. In fact, did he still need his brothers ? Wasn't it they who now found themselves in need ? He could have said, « God is with me, as you can see. Now it's they who are in trouble. It serves them right! » He could also have avenged himself and made them pay (he had both the power and the opportunity to do so – he was no longer the helpless victim). But Joseph preferred to listen to God and to put into practice what the Holy Spirit taught him.

Genesis 42:9

> And Joseph remembered the dreams which he dreamed of them.

No, Joseph had not forgotten the dreams which God had given him in his youth, and he had treasured God's promises. God's plan remained within him, more alive than ever.

4.5 - Genesis 42:7-15

> Even if Joseph's reaction seemed cold, his heart was not.

However, we could question the state of his brothers' consciences. The most serious harm is the death of the conscience. Joseph's brothers had had no scruples about killing their brother, nor selling him, nor lying to their father for years. They had silenced and then extinguished their conscience, and had become hardened and calloused. Thus it is, when the conscience is frozen and completely hardened, that it takes time to be awakened. Would Joseph succeed in awakening it ? He would not make himself known before their conscience was awakened. Though it may be difficult to wake up a sleeping conscience, it is nevertheless not impossible. The Holy Spirit will be the one to do it, because *what is impossible with men is possible with God.*

Do you want to receive a revelation about Jesus ? Your conscience, your soul must be resensitized, reawakened. The brothers needed to reflect upon themselves in order to recover their memory and a new sensitivity. Joseph's tests would reveal, one after the other, the hardness of their hearts. You could say these were some tough nuts to crack !

Test 1: The need to learn humility

The famine was part of this test. They had to leave the Promised Land and become dependents of another country whose gods were not the God of Israel. The self-sufficiency and spiritual pride of the patriarchs had to be set aside. They had to learn humility at the time when they no longer had much under their control. Although strong together (they were eleven, let us remember), they now had to depend upon Egypt and upon Joseph, the one whom they had, in their pride, kicked off of their team. This is Lesson Number One.

1 Peter 5:5

> God rejects the proud, but gives grace to the humble.

If we want to encounter the Lord, humility is a non-negotiable for awakening our hearts.

Test 2: The need to learn that we reap what we sow

Genesis 42:13-14

> And they said « your servants are twelve brothers, the sons of one man in the land of Canaan, and behold, the youngest is this day with our father, and one is no more. » And Joseph said unto them, « It is as I told you. You are spies! »

Joseph, recognizing them, spoke harshly to them, although his heart was broken. Now it was their turn to be judged wrongly. They are accused of being spies, although they had done nothing wrong. They had mistreated their brother, and now they were being mistreated. Their regret is evident in their tone, and they had forgotten nothing (« and one is no more »). They had to learn, sooner or later, that we reap what we sow. Not always in the same measure, thankfully – for God is a God of grace – but the principle remains.

Test 3: The need to recognize the wrong that had been done

Genesis 42:21-22

> They said to one another, « Surely we are being punished because of our brother. We saw how distressed he was when he pleaded with us for his life, but we would not listen; that's why this distress has come upon us. Reuben replied, « Didn't I tell you not to sin against the boy ? But you would not listen! Now we must give an accounting for his blood. »

Their memory was refreshed, and suddenly they could remember the exact conversation which transpired. All at once, Joseph's face was right there, jumping out at them. They could hear him cry out for mercy. The righteous guilt was beginning to take effect, and they lost all inner peace. The guilt which came from God was the root of their salvation. It has to do its work in order for us to be able to recognize the sin we have committed, and the need we have to be forgiven. When God forgives, he forgives completely, and there is no longer any condemnation for those who are in Christ Jesus.

Reuben felt responsible, his words betraying the growing anguish he feels. Yes, God had seen it all, and they would all be judged. It was horrifying.

Genesis 42:24

> Then he turned away from them and wept.

Joseph observed all of this and drew away, unable to hold back his tears. The brothers' outer shell was beginning to crack. Joseph had the power to save them from their emotional distress in a single moment, but the time was not yet right – for the work of the Holy Spirit needed to be accomplished thoroughly and completely. Sometimes we are in a rush to see people convert, and we forget that God has his own time, and that the work is being accomplished. Have patience, and trust. We want to say, « Ok, ok, the brothers have understood the error of their ways, » but in reality, they are not yet ready – although the moment is near. The reason that some Christians backslide shortly after their conversion is that they are truly touched, but have not come to a true and deep state of repentance.

Genesis 42:25

> Joseph gave orders to fill their bags with grain, to put each man's silver back in his sack, and to give them provisions for their journey. After this was done for them, they loaded their grain on their donkeys and left.

They departed with the grain they had purchased, but Joseph's men had put their money back into their sacks (evoking the memory of having sold their brother to the Midianite traders). This inexplicable occurrence led them to recognize their faults. The sight of that money in their sacks must have refreshed their memory !

Genesis 42:27-28

> At the place where they stopped for the night one of them opened his sack to get feed for his donkey, and he saw his silver in the mouth of his sack. « My silver has been returned » he said to his brothers. « Here it is in my sack. » Their hearts sank and they turned to each other trembling and said, « **What is this, that God has done to us? »**

What a conclusion to have come to! Instead of recognizing their wrongdoing, they accused the Lord! They had not yet « come to their senses » (Luke 15 :17). Instead of saying « What has God done to us ? » they ought to have been asking themselves, « What have we done to find ourselves here ? » They definitely recognized that something was not as it should be, that their past had resurfaced, and yet they accused God. Such erroneous judgment – they still had a bit more journeying to do.

Test 4: The need to understand grace

Genesis 43, the brothers' second journey.

Jacob was troubled by this unfolding story. Simeon had stayed in Egypt under the condition that his brothers would come back with Benjamin. As time went by, and provisions dwindled, they found themselves with no choice but to go back down to Egypt. Jacob was desperate. From their first entrance in Egypt, Joseph's hospitality had absolutely bewildered his brothers ; they had been welcomed with such grace and good will. They hardly understood anything anymore !

Romans 2:4

> God's kindness leads us to repentance.

In Genesis 44, Joseph struck a sensitive spot: the innocent son. Having turned back towards Canaan with a fresh cargo of wheat, each man's money had been returned to him, along with – as a bonus – Joseph's cup, which was found among Benjamin's belongings. Confusion and tension were at their peak. Benjamin was to remain in Egypt as a slave, which was precisely the sensitive spot that Joseph had wanted to hit.

Genesis 44:16

> God has uncovered your servants' guilt.

4.6 – Judah advocated

Genesis 44:32-34

> Your servant guaranteed the boy's safety to my father...Do not let me see the misery that would come upon my father.

Here we find ourselves in the thick of this highly emotional text; it was at this point that Joseph finally gave in. He knew that his brothers who had unscrupulously sold him were now prepared to defend their younger brother and even give their lives for him. They – insensitive, hardened, and cold – were now full of consideration, ready to do anything to save their younger brother. Judah was even prepared to take his place. They knew that they had lied to their father for all of those years – far too many of them – and they could not bear to see their father suffer any more. They were at rock bottom, prepared to give up everything they had. They were ripe for conversion, and for Joseph to reveal himself to them.

4.7 - The brothers were persuaded

They needed to feel their despair deep within their souls. In order to realize the wickedness we are capable of, we need to have a deep awareness. This is the path of repentance:« Father, I have sinned against heaven and against you » (Luke 15 :21).

The Lord has the ability to break through to all of us, to convince us, to touch our sensitive spot. Let us ask ourselves this question: « Who is this innocent son, whom the Father let go of with great sorrow ? » Like Jacob, God said « I cannot let go of my son », and yet it was the only way that He could reach us. The innocent son was « released» by the Father in order that we might be able to say, in this famished, desert land, « I do not want to grieve my Father any longer. I no longer want to hurt the beloved son, but I will welcome him and receive him. » Herein we find the message of the

Gospel:the Father gives his beloved Son for our salvation.

Next, the Lord will help us forget our painful past, to the extent that we say « yes » to forgiveness and « no » to bitterness. And if my past does try to resurface, I will be ready to face it because my heart is filled with the Lord. Like Joseph I will be able to cry for my brothers, but also for my enemies – for those who have wronged me – even twenty years down the road. For this, we must have the help of the Holy Spirit. We have to have experienced healing in the deepest part of our heart.

4.8 – Conclusion

Let us summarize the essential points of this message :

- Even a painful past will be stripped of its power to destroy, because *God has caused us to forget.*

- After Manasseh, may we allow Ephraim to be born in the depths of our heart, remaining fruitful in our lives despite affliction. May we practice forgiveness and reject bitterness.

- Let us guard our hearts above all else, being ready to « weep » for those who wrong us.

- The beloved son needed to leave the father, for the cross is the powerful means which God uses to touch our hearts and speak to us of the power of his love and forgiveness, of his righteousness and holiness. How can we remain unmoved when we touch the son of God ? Like Judah, are we prepared to give our lives for him ?

- Finally, let us note that it was true repentance which led to Joseph's revealing himself to his brothers.

- V -

Joseph reveals himself – Jacob rises again

We find ourselves perched on the brink of the climax. A miraculous restoration of relationships is about to take place, after twenty years of separation.

5.1 - Joseph, a type of Christ

Like Joseph, Christ was the beloved of the Father. He was sold by his brothers and became a slave (Philippians 2:7-8). He knew great pain, and is called the man of sorrows (Isaiah 53). He was characterized by his obedience to God (John 4:34, 8:29). Wrongly accused (Matthew 26:60), He was thrown into darkness (Matthew 27:45). The cupbearer and the baker bring to mind the two criminals on the cross (Luke 23:43). Joseph's emergence from prison is the very image of the resurrection (Romans 6:4). In Him are found all treasures of wisdom and revelation. He receives a bride who shares his glory (Ephesians 5:25-27). He receives power and dominion (Ephesians 1:20-22).

In the story of Joseph's life, those who let him lead were blessed in return. Such was the case with Potiphar. As it is written, « The LORD blessed the household of the Egyptian because of Joseph. The blessing of the LORD was on everything Potiphar had » (Genesis 39:5). When Pharaoh gave the highest position (after himself) to Joseph, all of Egypt was richly blessed and saved from famine. It is the same for us. If we give Jesus Christ the highest place in our lives, we are richly blessed because of it. If we refuse him, we suffer an immense loss – both in this world and in the next. Let us seek to know, therefore, how to grant him the highest place in our lives.

Jesus is not only the savior of His people, however; He is the Savior of the world. He was never consumed by bitterness or hatred, resentment or vengeance. Joseph's character was shaped by numerous trials, and he became a man of honor, integrity, righteousness, peace, and compassion – in the image of Jesus.

He had not forgotten his dreams. He did not forget the word of God, and the time of accomplishment was at hand. The famine would bring everyone together, and the past would be set right. God himself was taking care of Joseph, and accomplishing a profound work in his life.

Before revealing himself, Joseph decided to test his brothers to determine the true state of their hearts. (Had they changed over the course of the past twenty years ?) Without deep repentance, communion could never be restored. In the end, the climax came when Joseph demanded the youngest brother, the innocent son. This is what brought the brothers to the end of themselves, because he threatened to take what was most precious to their father. Judah, out of love for his elderly father, could no longer continue to see him unhappy, and so made a declaration and confession which would have pierced even the hardest heart. How much more must Joseph have been touched! *« And God will pour out a spirit of grace upon his people, and they will look upon him whom they have pierced! »* (Zechariah 12 :10).

5.2 - Joseph revealed himself: Genesis 45:1-8

We discover the message of the Gospel in this chapter, because this text is prophetic in nature. Just like Joseph, who made everyone leave in order to be alone with his brothers, I believe that the Lord Jesus, the Messiah, after having poured out a spirit of grace and supplication upon his people (as per the prophet Zechariah), is going to reveal himself to them personally. (They will look upon him whom they have pierced.) We pray that this spirit of grace and supplication may come upon the chosen people of God, because their story is tied to our story. What Israel will experience is tied to the history of the world, and the world is tied to Israel's story. This is why we pray for the conversion of God's chosen people – that is, Jesus' brothers – and for them to recognize the Messiah. Let us examine the text a little more closely:

v. 3 – I am Joseph! You thought me dead, but it was not true. Your sin « crucified » me but I have overcome. I have good news for you: I reign in Egypt, every storehouse is full, and the provisions are there for you. Joseph did not take just any moment to reveal himself to them, but rather chose the moment of their repentance.

v. 4 – Come close to me. This is exactly what Jesus is saying to us today. « I am not dead, but alive. I will not shun him who draws near to me. My heritage is for you.

v. 5 – God sent me ahead of you to **save lives**. That is, that you might live. Joseph will tell them this three different times: see thus how Joseph speaks to his former enemies. May we imitate this. We find ourselves, here, at the very heart of the message of the Gospel (Matthew 5:44 – *Love your enemies*).

Sometimes we would prefer that God remove our enemies, take them out of harm's way, or even destroy them; but we are called to put into practice the Sermon on the Mount: love, bless, and allow HIS power to manifest itself.

What is an enemy? Someone who prevents me from entering into my calling. It could be a bad habit, a recurring problem, an obstacle, a trial, a person, or a group of people. Yet, paradoxically, the « enemy » forces us to cope and move forward in our Christian walk.

Mike Murdock once said, « you have no future without an enemy. » It was because of Goliath, the enemy of Israel, that David was introduced onto the scene that great day. Without him, he would have remained an anonymous little shepherd. In a single day, David broke the yoke which had burdened his people, gained access to the royal palace, and married the daughter of the king! Yes, the enemy's existence requires us to be vigilant, to watch and pray, to guard our hearts and keep them pure before the Lord, and to cling to God.

We must trust in the power of prayer. If the enemy is weighing me down, it is in order that I may learn how to fight. Your enemies, without realizing it, are propelling you towards your destiny. Without knowing it, those who would try to « throw you in the well » are the very instruments who will speed you on your way to the palace, before the throne of grace. In rejecting you, they push you into the eternal arms of God, because it is in turning towards him that you find strength and comfort. Some will crucify you, but in doing so they are unaware that you will be resurrected. You will find the strength of God working in you and through you, which will be the very key to victory.

Genesis 50:20

> You intended to harm me, but God intended it for good to accomplish what is now being done, the saving of many lives.

Upon looking a little more closely, you perceive that those who intended to harm you have actually pushed you a little further towards your destiny in Christ. God changes bad into good by transforming the heart. As soon as you grasp this truth, you will begin to love your enemies and bless God for those who curse you. We would want God to work on our enemies, but God says « I am going to work on YOU », to fashion your heart and your character in order that you may enter into your calling.

5.3 - Joseph forgave his brothers: Genesis 45:17-18

Joseph invited his brothers to his home. Pharaoh was evidently in favor of family reunification, because he encouraged his prime minister, Joseph, to invite his entire family, and also saw to it that they would have whatever they needed.

We could ask ourselves if Joseph had truly forgiven his brothers. To do and say these kinds of things, it is evident that Joseph had indeed forgiven them. He was no longer continually tormented by the evil which they had done to him. Perhaps this had taken him some time, but at a given point he had been liberated, his heart had been calmed. The Christian knows that he must forgive because the Word of God is crystal clear:if you do not forgive, you have a problem with God! We « have to forgive » because no one wants to miss the boat to heaven due to unforgiveness, but this is just the beginning. What is required is forgiving with all your heart; Jesus does not tolerate superficial forgiveness, granted merely to save your own skin !

Let us note that Joseph forgave his brothers without expecting anything in return. Injured, we often expect something from the other person: repentance, recognition of wrongs committed. This prevents us from being truly free. To be able to weep and show compassion at this moment, Joseph had manifestly forgiven them with all his heart, like Jesus. (« Father, forgive them, for they know not what they do. ») However, to be able to rediscover a relationship with the Lord, we must ask forgiveness. Forgiveness is liberating. Nevertheless, to restore broken relationships it is imperative that forgiveness be asked. The brothers had to do it eventually, but Joseph had not required anything from them.

If we read Genesis 50:16 – 21, we observe that Jacob, before dying, had *commanded* his sons to ask forgiveness. Their spiritual maturity was not what Joseph's was. Notice that their attempts were mixed with the fear that Joseph might one day turn against them (v. 15).

Joseph went to great lengths in his steps toward forgiveness. He even went so far as to console his aggressors. They were tormented by their guilt, burdened by the gravity of their acts. Joseph mentioned nothing but the essential thing for him: God had been in charge of everything! He then went still further: encouraged by the words of Pharaoh, he wanted to spend the rest of his life in their company, and invited them to his home. It did not bother him that they would receive the best part of the land. They did not deserve anything, but were covered by grace. This is what the Bible means when it says to « bless your enemies. »

Romans 12:18-21

> If it is possible, as far as it depends on you, live at peace with everyone...If your enemy is hungry, feed him ; if he is thirsty, give him something to drink. In doing this, you will heap burning coals on his head. Do not be overcome by evil, but overcome evil with good.

Let us leave a door open for reconciliation, and for the restoration of relationships.

5.4 - Jacob rose again: Genesis 45:21-28

Joseph wanted to see his father again. In chapters 42 to 44, he asked multiple times for news of his father. Was he still alive? Was he in good health? His true pain was the emptiness left by the absence of his father and his younger brother. When he saw Benjamin, he was « deeply moved » (Genesis 43:30) and left the room to weep. (Something very strong bound them together:they had the same mother, Rachel, who had died when giving birth to Benjamin. Benjamin was also the only one who had not participated in the brothers' conspiracy to sell Joseph.)

5.5 - Jacob's heart remained cold

Joseph charged his brothers with delivering a very important message: « I am alive! I rule over all of Egypt. I will open my storehouses for you. (v. 9) Make haste and come down to me. I have the best in Egypt for you – I will feed you. Tell my father of all the honor accorded me here » (v. 13).

Joseph's brothers were hardly reliable witnesses. Could they even be believed, they who had lied for twenty years? Could the good news which they tried to bring to poor old Jacob be taken seriously? Jacob was no fool; he had known many others. He no longer believed them, but was skeptical, distrusting, indifferent, aged, and no longer even knew how to feel. He had cried enough over his lost son and his wife Rachel. He had no more tears left for pranks! His life was broken; his heart, cold. He was more or less « dead » due to the bad news that he had believed during all these years. His life just then consisted of suffering under the weight of the years, and waiting for the end. Lot had also been a poor witness: when he asked his family to depart from Sodom (upon the order of angels), the Bible says that his sons-in-law took this affair for a joke! Lot was no longer credible.

Joseph's brothers were bringing news that was true, but they were no longer believable. The message they were bringing was precious, but we can see that their lives were no longer credible. Our words and our lives should be mutually affirming, because words are not enough. How many people know only the bad news! They have only ever heard this message alone. What must we do? How can we awaken their hearts?

5.6 - Joseph's carts revived Jacob's spirit

Genesis 45:27

> Jacob saw the carts that Joseph had sent to carry him back.

God's response to this problem is the carts from Joseph, loaded with gifts, bearing unmistakeable signs that his son was alive and well. What touches the heart of one who can no longer believe (who has known only pain and bad news) is when the Lord says, « I am preparing a table before you, preparing my riches before you. I am opening your heart so that you may see what I have done for you. » The Son himself comes to our aid to reveal himself.

What do the carts represent ?

v. 23: ten donkeys loaded with the best things of Egypt, and ten female donkeys...

These are pieces of evidence bearing witness to the change in Joseph's situation. Something denoting the richness, life, blessing, and power of God ought to mark and accompany our lives, otherwise it will carry no weight. (A changed life will produce a transformed character, showing signs of joy, peace, zeal, and love.) Only these signs of God will be able to convince the unbelieving; they are necessary to awaken sleeping hearts.

Mark 16:17, 20

> And these signs will accompany those who believe...and the Lord worked with them and confirmed his word by the signs that accompanied it.

The carts are representative of abundance.

Psalm 34:9

> Taste and see that the Lord is good.

5.7 - Jacob became Israel once more

Genesis 45:27 - 46:1

> But when they told him everything Joseph had said to them, and when he saw the carts Joseph had sent to carry him back, the spirit of their father **Jacob** revived. And **Israel** said, « I am convinced! My son Joseph is still alive. I will go and see him before I die. » So Israel set out with all that was his, and when he reached Beersheba, he offered sacrifices to the God of his father Isaac.

Notice: JACOB saw the carts, and his spirit revived. Then, ISRAEL spoke. Jacob received a personal and individualized testimony from the son whom he believed dead. The Bible first calls him Jacob, but the person who would rise up in faith and accept this message, believing it, is here called by the name *Israel*. He is most certainly the same person.

Jacob means « supplanter » or « one who tricks » and he himself was indeed deceived in his own turn. But the Lord said « you shall no longer be called Jacob ; you shall be called Israel. This is a new name I am giving you, the new person that you shall be. » The first of a new people. He arose and left his years of depression behind him. He was no longer subject to his circumstances, but chose his own path; he did not stay lying down in defeat, nor stuck in the past, but got up and literally returned to life!

You also are a Jacob called to live as an Israel. Get up by the power of the new person who is within you! Jacob's life took a twist, and his ministry was reborn from the ashes. He came back to life and **worshiped** (at Beersheba), then had a **vision** (46 :2). God **spoke** to him. As soon as he arrived in Egypt, he **blessed** Pharaoh as well as the children of Joseph. He was filled with discernment and blessings for his descendants, and prophesied over the twelve tribes.

Genesis 48:15

> God has been my shepherd all my life to this day.

Jacob had made so many mistakes in his life, and known so much distress, but God had always watched over him.

Psalm 23:4

> Even though I walk through the valley of the shadow of death, I will fear no evil, for you are with me. Your rod and your staff, they comfort me.

God comforts him. What a glorious ending for this life!

- VI -
Running over walls

6.1 - Jacob's awakening

Genesis 45:28

> And Israel said, « That's enough! My son Joseph is alive. I will go and see him before I die. »

What Joseph's brothers were incapable of doing, his carts would accomplish. They were the signs of his goodness and warmth, evidence of his ardent desire to see his aged father again (which is itself an image of God's goodness, and the way he issues us a personal invitation). The proof of the carts revived Jacob's dormant heart, and it was Israel who got up, departed, and arrived at Beersheba (a place of revelation). Although eager to join his son, Israel needed a confirmation from God. He was serious about his quest. He wanted to make sure that it was correct, and was in need of reassurance. His fathers before him, Abraham and Isaac, had already gone down to Egypt against the will of God, and things had not gone well. Thus Jacob paused: he needed to get the green light from God.

Genesis 46:3

> Do not be afraid to go down to Egypt.

It is so important to keep ourselves from paths in which we are likely to be deceived. It is absolutely crucial to have peace in our hearts.

6.2 - Jacob's faith

Hebrews 11:21

> **By faith** Jacob, when he was dying, **blessed** each of Joseph's sons, and worshipped as he leaned on the top of his staff.

Jacob would say to Pharaoh: « I have lived 130 years, and my years have been few and difficult. » His faith suddenly found a new vigor, and he was thoroughly rejuvenated by the power of the Holy Spirit. The man was physically broken – he walked with a limp – but he had never walked so well with God. He was practically blind, but his spiritual vision had never been so clear! We find here a man broken, and yet spiritually powerful.

May we not be afraid of our physical weakness, as long as our soul is alive. The deepest desire of Jacob's heart, now that they were all reunited in Egypt, was to *bless*. May it be the same for us: let us bless as large an area as possible (our families, our posterity). Our blessing will have an influence, as had that of Jacob, but only insofar as we offer it in **faith**. *By faith Jacob blessed*, and the words that he pronounced would have prophetic weight and impact. Never cease to bless your offspring. There will be no limit to the blessing. Your prayers shall be heard.

Genesis 49:28

> All these are the twelve tribes of Israel, and this is what their father said to them when he **blessed** them, giving each the **blessing** appropriate to him.

With great precision he gave a word to each one of his sons. He discerned that Joseph's two sons would be on an equal level with his own sons. He would give a double portion to Joseph, placing Manasseh and Ephraim on the same step, next to the other sons, because of the rights of the firstborn.

6.3 - All of God's word shall be accomplished

God had not forgotten Joseph's dreams, those dreams which He himself had inspired. People might have said « It is just vanity, lies. You're making things up. That's just a human invention. » But God does not forget the Word which he himself has given. Do not doubt it! God will cause this word to resurge and come back to life. What God declares will indeed be accomplished, even twenty years after the fact. This is precisely what released the hatred of Joseph's brothers. We see that the will of God is contested by the enemy. There is such a thing as spiritual warfare. May we not forget what the Lord has sown in our hearts. His word shall not perish – all will be accomplished.

Joseph's **bones** would go out of Egypt, an image of the resurrection.

Genesis 50:24-25

> Joseph said to his brothers, « I am about to die. But God will surely come to your aid and take you up out of this land to the land he promised on oath to Abraham, Isaac, and Jacob. And Joseph made the Israelites swear an oath and said « God will surely come to your aid, and then you must **carry my bones up from this place**. » (400 years later)

Exodus 13:19

> **Moses** took the bones of Joseph with him because Joseph had made the Israelites swear an oath. He had said, « God will surely come to your aid, and then you must carry my bones up with you from this place. »

Joseph knew that later on his entire tribe, all his descendants, would go back up to Canaan. This reminds us that nothing is destined to remain in the foreign land in which we are residing, but that everything must depart for the Promised Land. There is even hope for our bones! It is the hope of the resurrection. Genesis ends with the death of Joseph, at 110 years old, and they embalmed him in Egypt. God remembered Joseph's bones. In the first book of the Bible we already find hope for the resurrection of the body.

Psalm 16:10-11

You will not abandon my soul to the realm of the dead, nor will you let your faithful one see decay. You will show me the path of life; in your presence is fullness of joy. At your right hand are pleasures forevermore.

Daniel 12:2

Multitudes who sleep in the dust of the earth will awake: some to everlasting life, others to shame and everlasting contempt.

John 5:28-29

For a time is coming when all who are in their graves will hear his voice and come out – those who have done what is good will rise to live, and those who have done what is evil will rise to be condemned.

The right of the firstborn

1 Chronicles 5:1-2

The sons of Reuben the firstborn of Israel (he was the firstborn, but when he defiled his father's marriage bed, his **rights as firstborn were given to the sons of Joseph** son of Israel; so he could not be listed in the genealogical record in accordance with his birthright, and though Judah was the strongest of his brothers and a ruler came from him, the rights of the firstborn belonged to Joseph.)

God gave Joseph the right of the firstborn – that is, a double portion, a double inheritance. Manasseh and Ephraim would be two great tribes who lived in a vast territory in which were many mountains, according to the prophecy of Jacob. He who had been rejected would be the firstborn in the eyes of his father and in the eyes of God, even if it was through the descendants of Judah that would come the Messiah – the King.

6.4 - Key Verse: God causes evil to work out for good (Genesis 50:20)

God not only changed evil into good, but he changed a man and his entire destiny.

6.5 - His branches climb over the wall

Genesis 49:22-26

> Joseph is a fruitful vine, a **fruitful vine near a spring**; whose branches climb over a wall. With bitterness archers attacked him; they shot at him with hostility. But his bow remained steady, his strong arms stayed limber, because of the hand of the Mighty One of Jacob, because of the Shepherd, the Rock of Israel, because of your father's God, who helps you, because of the Almighty who blesses you with blessings of the heavens above, blessings of the deep that lies below, blessings of the breast and womb. Your father's blessings are greater than the

> blessings of the ancient mountains, than the bounty of the age-old hills. Let all these rest on the head of Joseph, on the brow of the prince among his brothers.

It was Joseph who was blessed beyond measure. Even Judah, the royal tribe, would not receive such a blessing!

Once there was a father and his son who lived in peace and harmony upon the earth. They worked together and lived off of the fruit of their labor. They shared everything until the day when conflict erupted. It all began with a small difference of opinion and a misunderstanding. Their relationship weakened little by little, and a distance appeared between them. The gap grew little by little until, one day, a heated discussion exploded between them. Taking their positions firmly, a painful silence settled upon them both. For months they no longer spoke to one another. One day someone knocked at the door of the son. It was a handyman looking for work :

- « Do you have any repairs that need doing ? »
- « Yes, he responded, I have some work for you. You see, on the other side of this brook lives my father. Several months ago he hurt me very badly, and our relationship is broken. I am going to show him that I can do without him. Do you see these stones beside my house ? I want you to build a wall two meters high, because I don't want to see him any longer! »

The man responded:

- « I think I understand. » The son helped his visitor to collect all the necessary material. Then he went away on his travels, leaving him on his own for a week. When the son returned, the man had already finished his work. But what a surprise! The son was completely taken aback. Instead of a wall two meters high, he had built a magnificent bridge. Just then, the father came out of house and ran towards his son exclaiming,

- « You are incredible! To build a bridge after what I did to you! I am proud of you, and ask for your forgiveness. »

While the father and his son celebrated their reconciliation, the handyman was gathering his tools to leave.

- « No, wait! They said to him. There is work here for you! »

But he responded, « I would certainly like to stay, but I still have other bridges to build. »

The word of God says that Joseph kept his heart from hardness, vengeance, hatred, and bitterness. Thanks to this it was possible to « build a bridge » which permitted the very plan of God to be accomplished (that is, the entire nation of Israel came to Egypt). The prophecy said that Joseph was surrounded by a wall, and that this wall intended to close him in, imprison him, and damage his life. These were nothing but dead-end situations: thrown into a well, robbed of his freedom, slandered, falsely accused, thrown into prison, forgotten in his dungeon cell. They had planned to take everything from him, but God had in fact added to his life.

Instead of spiraling downward into sadness or depression, he rose up. There will always be walls to imprison us: circumstances, words, and attitudes which will erect barriers in our lives and try to stop us in our tracks. Instead of descending into defeat, doubt, or unbelief, we must « rise up » and overcome, climbing over these walls.

Psalm 18:29

> With my God I can **scale** a wall.

Zechariah 4:6-7

> Then he said to me, « This is the word of the LORD to Zerubbabel: « Not by might, nor by power, but by my Spirit, says the LORD of hosts. **Who are you, O great mountain ? Before Zerubbabel you shall become a plain.**

Who are you, O high wall before me ? You shall be knocked down.

Psalm 105:18-19

> They bruised his feet with shackles, his neck was put in irons, till what he foretold came to pass, till the word of the LORD proved him true.

God can bring down walls, and he can also cause us to climb over them. God opens a path and lifts us up above the wall, by his strength. How ?

Joseph is a fruitful vine near a spring (Genesis 49:22).

Psalm 1

> Blessed is the man...whose delight is in the law of the Lord, and on His law he meditates day and night. He is like a **tree planted by streams of water**, which yields its fruit in season, and whose leaf does not wither. Everything he does prospers.

Jeremiah 17:7

> But blessed is the man who trusts in the LORD, whose confidence is in him. He will be like a **tree planted by the water** that sends out its roots by the stream. It does not fear when heat comes: its leaves are always green. It has no worries in a year of drought and never fails to bear fruit.

The streams of water are not far off! Joseph plunged his roots down deep into the foundation of faith. He grew and became « the shepherd and the rock of Israel » (Genesis 49:24). He didn't change suddenly from one instant to the next, but he **became**. By drawing his strength from this deepest source, his tree grew and Joseph rose above to become a reference, a shepherd, a column, a support, a rock for all of Israel, a man seen and known by everyone, one of those that would never be forgotten: his branches climbed over the wall.

This is how God shapes his servants and gives birth to ministries. Let us remember this quote from Mike Murdoch: « You have no future without an enemy! »

Your enemies, without realizing it, are actually pushing you towards your destiny. Through the course of his trials, Joseph was obliged to grow even stronger in order to survive.

Israel's future is to climb over the wall

Beyond geographic borders, beyond limits, Israel shall be a blessing which will spread out into foreign nations according to the promises of God. The time is at hand! In the same way, the task of the church is to bear fruit which will be « exported » abroad (see Galatians 5, on the fruit of the Spirit). For example: the fruit of wisdom, compassion, forgiveness, prayer, service.

Christ, by his resurrection, was raised up above the wall of death and gives us a share in His resurrection. In His ascension, He was raised above every wall and He reigns in Heaven. It is when we are **united with Christ** that we share in His destiny. Christ sweeps us up into His victory – we are seated with Him in the heavenly realms (Ephesians 2:6). Friend, you are blessed with every spiritual blessing in the heavenly places (Ephesians 1:3).

Blessings of the heavens above (or from the heavens on high) which come from the Lord. This is where He is, and from where He blesses us (Acts 2:33). As well as *blessings of the deep* (or from the waters below) which come from our trials. Jesus descended into the depths where the dead sojourn, and rose again from there (Romans 10:7). He set the captives free, and conquered every power below, and the princes of the kingdom of darkness (Colossians 2:15). Glory to God!

Table of contents

- V - 57

Joseph reveals himself – Jacob rises again 57

- VI - 69

Running over walls 69

www.ingramcontent.com/pod-product-compliance
Ingram Content Group UK Ltd.
Pitfield, Milton Keynes, MK11 3LW, UK
UKHW020237250726
13967UKWH00001B/423